Marina Heilmeyer

The Language of Flowers

Symbols and Myths

Prestel

Munich · Berlin · London · New York

A look at the centuries-old relationship between flowers and their admirers

"Oh, Tiger-lily," said Alice, addressing herself to one that was gracefully waving in the wind, "I wish you could talk!" "We can talk," said the Tiger-lily, "when there's anybody worth talking to."

When, in 1872, Lewis Carroll sent Alice through the looking glass into the garden of talking flowers, the debate surrounding the soul and the language of flowers had already reached its climax and begun to wane. It had been prompted by the 1761 publication of J.-J. Rousseau's novel *Julie, ou la Nouvelle Héloïse* (Julie, or the new Eloise). 'Feeling' as a spiritual dimension had been rediscovered and a lively appreciation of beauty in nature was intended to instil a sense of morality and piety.

The question first asked by Aristotle as to whether plants had a soul or not was duly rekindled. He had drafted a hierarchy of living things that placed plants between inanimate nature and animals, attributing them with their own specific type of soul, despite their inability to move.

Historic documents indicate that considerable time has been devoted to the essence and effects of plants from very early times. Despite the danger and hard work this involved, persistent investigation continued into the beneficial or detrimental effects of plants on the human body and mind.

Plants seemed to be capable of transferring divine power. The ancient Egyptians believed that the gods used flowers to infuse mankind with positive energy. Fragrant flowers thus played an essential role in all festivities and rituals. The inhabitants of ancient Greece also believed that the scent of a flower preceded the imminent apparition of a god.

The more rational philosophers of imperial Rome on the other hand feared that strong scent would cloud their vision and powers of judgement. Nevertheless, the Romans made extravagant use of flowers, carpeting whole rooms with rose petals or fragrant saffron crocuses. This is why early Christians regarded flowers as symbols of 'decadent' pagan culture.

Under the increased influence of Islamic thought, which maintained that the beauty of each flower is a symbol of God's spirit, Christianity also eventually reinterpreted the symbolism of flowers to suit its own beliefs. The spell had now been broken, and the culture, symbolism and language of flowers developed rapidly.

In the early romances of the Middle Ages, the garden was the favourite setting for love stories and illustrations show posies being lovingly bound and exchanged in flower gardens.

Flowers became the messengers of feelings. Intimacies were exchanged in a figurative, round-about way and every educated person understood what message was being sent if presented with a certain type of posy. Tear-stained roses became symbols of love and pain.

The mid-sixteenth century marked the beginning of an incredibly rapid transformation in Europe within the world of plants. From 1556 onwards, bulbs of magnificent new flowers were shipped in from the Orient, especially tulips. Soon, even more new varieties were brought back from the New World. The tremendous success enjoyed by Ovid's *Metamorphoses* around this time is probably because it made a poetic attempt to idealise the transformations and changes which people were experiencing. This was the age of the Reformation and Counter-Reformation. It was believed that God's wishes were clearly manifested in creation. Every flower had a hidden message. Attuned observers could interpret this and draw moral conclusions. Roses, for instance, exude the sweet perfume of virtue, sunflowers bless all actions performed in accordance with God's will, blue hyacinths encourage us to meditate on God and heaven, while the crown imperial reminds us of the futility of human power.

Many seventeenth-century flower paintings have a specific moral and religious intention: optimistic observers recognised God's loving kindness in the beauty of flowers, while more serious thinkers were transported to a meditative realm. Newly introduced flowers, such as the sunflower, were immediately integrated into this network of symbolism.

This genre of symbolism underwent radical change with the coming of the Enlightenment. Far removed from the moral lessons imparted by Baroque bouquets, eighteenth century posies conveyed personal sentiments and messages from the heart.

The concept of a 'language of flowers' first became popular in the nineteenth century, although it had already been documented in reports written by travellers to the Orient, published in France as early as 1680. These manuscripts describe a secret flower code used by ladies in eastern harems to express their desires or feelings. These ideas developed and 1818 saw the publication in France of the first book about the language of flowers, a reference book on floral symbolism that opened up a whole new world to spellbound readers. As in previous centuries, this reference work was based on older sources, namely the literature of antiquity, the ensuing Christian symbolism, the Minnesinger's works that had recently been rediscovered and the romances of the Middle Ages.

In the salons of the bourgeoisie, attempts were made to play with these symbols and to awaken or express feelings, and floral 'dictionaries' were often kept at close hand for immediate consultation on the receipt of specific posies. Flowers were now 'messengers of the heart' and played a significant role expressing feelings, or when joyful or sad news had to be delivered. Colour was also associated with certain qualities. For centuries, red roses have been a symbol of love and affection, white lilies symbolise the epitome of purity and blue flowers suggest faithfulness and romance. Today our writing can still be elaborately 'flowery', even if all we want to do is to 'say it with flowers'.

The following pages provide an insight into the 'language' of significant flowers such as roses, tulips and carnations, as well as other well-loved varieties.

*T*he Flowers

Peter Snijers, *The Month of April*, 1727,
Musées royaux des Beaux-Arts de Belgique, Brussels

(For information on the paintings illustrated,
see pages 58-60).

Anemone

Anemone coronaria

Symbolic of fading youth,
suffering and death; the first
flower of the year, every
gardener's pride

The garden anemone
from *Curtis Botanical
Magazine*, 1791

Thistle

Silybum marianum

Scotland's national emblem;
a symbol of hard work, suffering and Christ's deliverance;
dispels melancholy

Inflorescence and root of
the milk thistle, 1828

Strawberry

Fragaria vesca

First fruit of the year; a symbol
of purity and sensuality,
fertility and abundance,
humility and modesty

Strawberry plant from
Versailles, 1787

Pomegranate

Punica granatum

Sensuous love and passion,
fertility and immortality;
intellectual ability and
creative power; a symbol
of compassion;
an aphrodisiac

Flower and fruit of the
pomegranate tree, 1828

Hyacinth

Hyacinthus orientalis

Intense fragrance; symbolises
death and revival; used to
delay sexual maturity

Flowers and bulbs
of the oriental hyacinth,
1845

I ris

Iris

A symbol of faith and authority;
victory and conquest but
also pain; a protection from
evil spirits

Flower and rootstock of
an iris, 1828

*H*oneysuckle

Lonicera caprifolium

Ravishing, sensuous fragrance; a symbol of lasting pleasure, permanence and steadfastness

Flower and fruit of the honeysuckle, 1840

Crown Imperial

Fritillaria imperialis

Majestic flower of the
high society; principal
ornament of stylish
sixteenth and seven-
teenth century gardens;
arrogance and pride

Flower of the Crown
Imperial, 1808

Camellia
Camellia japonica

The most sought-after and expensive flowers of the nineteenth century; a symbol of the transience of life; delicate and elegant

Flower and stamen of a camellia, 1787

Crocus

Crocus vernus · Crocus sativus

A symbol of the Resurrection and heavenly bliss; renowned relative saffron used as seasoning, medicine, aphrodisiac and dye

Five different species of crocus, 1690

Lily
Lilium candidum

Purity; the supreme
flower – exalted and
unapproachable; strong
religious symbolism;
powerful fragrance

Flower and bulb of the
Madonna lily, 1845

Lily of the Valley
Convallaria majalis

Fortune in love;
poisonous yet with
healing powers; a symbol
of the Virgin Mary;
making the right choice

Flower and fruit of the
lily of the valley, 1833

Daisy

Bellis perennis

The love flower; contempt
for worldly goods; a favourite
among lovers, poets and children

Pierre-Joseph Redouté,
Daisy, from *La Botanique
de J.-J. Rousseau*, 1805

Poppy

Papaver rhoeas · Papaver somniferum

Magical flower;
represents life and
death, good and evil,
light and darkness;
fruitfulness

Flower and multiple fruit
of the opium poppy,
1828

Daffodil

Narcissus pseudonarcissus · Narcissus poeticus

Vanity and death, resurrection and rebirth; the promise of eternal life; the flower of the underworld

Bulb and flower
of a daffodil, 1787

Carnation

Dianthus caryophyllus

Bravery, love and
friendship; vanity
and pride; socialism;
the symbol for
Mother's Day

Flowers of the
garden carnation, 1840

Passion Flower

Passiflora coerulea

Powerful symbol of the
suffering of Christ,
faith and suffering,
but also of primeval
nature; yearning for a
long-lost paradise

Blue passion flower,
1787

Rose
Rosa gallica

Love and joy; a paragon of
virtue; beauty and fragrance;
the queen of flowers; used
to treat headaches, hysteria
and other complaints

Provins Rose,
1828

Sunflower

Helianthus annuus

Vital source of food,
medicine and oil; natural
vitality; loyalty; pride;
devotion; inspiration
to van Gogh

Flower and stamen of the
sunflower, 1840

*T*ulip
Tulipa gesneriana

Object of wild speculation; a
symbol of vanitas but also of
spring; wealth and importance;
arrogant and aloof

Flower and bulb of the
wild tulip, 1809

Forget-me-not

Myosotis palustris

Sign of human longing for
loyalty and lastingness;
humility; medicinal properties

Flower and seed of the
marsh forget-me-not,
1840

Primula

Primula veris · P. auricula

Happiness and satis-
faction; contentment and
pleasure but also frivolity
and thoughtlessness

Scented primrose,
1840

Index of Works Illustrated

The details shown on these pages have been taken
from the following works:

Camillia pp. 2 and 31
Ferdinand Waldmüller, *Birthday Table*, 1840, oil on canvas,
Wallraf-Richartz-Museum, Cologne

Crocus p. 33
Ambrosius Bosschaert the Elder, *Bouquet of Flowers*,
1620, oil on canvas, Musée du Louvre, Paris

Lily p. 35
Balthasar van der Ast, *Still Life with Flowers and Fruit*,
c. 1640/50, oil on panel, Anhaltinische Gemäldegalerie
Dessau, Dessau

Lily of the Valley p. 37
Jacques de Gheyn, *Flowers in a Glass*, 1612,
oil on canvas, Haags Historisch Museum, The Hague

Daisy p. 39
Bellis perennis, from *Curtis Botanical Magazine*, no. 228,
vol. 7, 1793, Botanisches Museum, Berlin

Poppy p. 41
Jan Davidsz de Heem, *Bouquet of Flowers in a Glass Vase*,
c. 1640, oil on canvas, Gemäldegalerie, Staatliche Museen
zu Berlin, Preußischer Kulturbesitz, Berlin

Daffodil p. 43
Roelant Savery, Bouquet of Flowers, 1612,
oil on canvas, The Royal Collections, Liechtenstein

Carnation p. 45
Jacob Marrel, *Flower-Adorned Cartouche with a View of Frankfurt*,
1651, oil on panel, Historisches Museum
der Stadt Frankfurt am Main, Frankfurt

Passion Flower p. 47
Jan Frans van Dael, *Tomb of Julie*, 1803/04,
oil on canvas, Château de Malmaison et Bois-Préau,
Malmaison

Rose p. 49

Antoine Berjon, *Still Life with Flowers, Shells, a Shark's Head and Fossils*, 1819, oil on canvas, Philadelphia Museum of Art, purchased with the Edith H. Bell Fund

Sunflower p. 51

Jan Davidsz de Heem, *Fruit and Flower Cartouche with Wine Glass*, 1651, oil on canvas, Gemäldegalerie, Staatliche Museen zu Berlin Preußischer Kulturbesitz, Berlin

Tulip p. 53

Georg Flegel, *Two Tulips*, c. 1630, watercolour, Kupferstich-kabinett, Staatliche Museen zu Berlin Preußischer Kulturbesitz, Berlin

Forget-me-not p. 55

Balthasar van der Ast, *Still Life with Basket of Flowers*, 1640/50, oil on canvas, Statens Konstmur, Stockholm

Primula p. 57

Jan van Huysum, *Bouquet of Flowers in Front of a Park Landscape*, c. 1730, oil on canvas, Kunsthistorisches Museum, Vienna

Photographic Credits

Anders, Jörg P., Berlin pp. 17, 19, 23, 41, 51, 53
Cussac, G., Brussels p. 13
Wood, Graydon p. 49
Ziegenfusz, Horst p. 45

Antwerp, Koninklijk Museum voor schone Kunsten p. 21
Berlin, Botanischer Garten und Botanisches Museum p. 39
Cologne, Rheinisches Bildarchiv pp. 2, 31
Dessau, Anhaltinische Gemäldegalerie p. 35
Dresden, Gemäldegalerie Alte Meister p. 27
The Hague, Haags Historisch Museum p. 37

Paris, Réunion des Musées Nationaux: G. Blot/C. Jean p. 33;
    C. Jean p. 47
Peissenberg, Artothek Joachim Blauel p. 29
Saint-Etienne, Musée d'Art moderne de Saint-Etienne p. 15
Stockholm, The National Museum of Fine Art p. 55
Vaduz, Liechtenstein, The Royal Collections p. 43
Vienna, Kunsthistorisches Museum pp. 25, 57

The botanical illustrations have been taken from the following works:

Anckelmann, Caspar, *Blumenbuch* (Horti Anckelmanniani I.),
    c. 1700 (Kupferstichkabinett, Staatliche Museen zu Berlin
    Preußischer Kulturbesitz, Berlin)
Curtis Botanical Magazine, 1787–1839
Schlechtendal, Diedrich Franz Leonhard von, *Flora von
    Deutschland*, Jena 1840–73
Reichenbach, Heinrich Gottlieb Ludwig, *Deutschlands Flora*,
    1837–50
Dietrichs, Ludwig Michael, *Flora des Königreichs Preußen*
Nees von Esenbeck, Theodor Friedrich Ludwig, *Plantae officinalis
    oder Sammlung offizineller Pflanzen* ·
(all four above titles from: Botanischer Garten und Botanisches
    Museum, Berlin)
Rousseau, Jean-Jacques, *La Botanique*, illustrated by Pierre-Joseph
    Redouté, 1805

With special thanks to
Dietrich Roth, Hamburg,
for providing the illustrations
on pp. 15 and 33

Front cover: Rose, aquilegia and lemon
Frontispiece: Ferdinand Waldmüller, *Birthday Table*, 1840 (see p. 31)
Page 4: Sandro Botticelli, *La Primavera – The Spring* (detail), 1482,
Uffizi, Florence

The Library of Congress Cataloguing-in-Publication data is available.
British Library Cataloguing-in-Publication Data: a catalogue record
for this book is available from the British Library; Die Deutsche Bibliothek
holds a record of this publication in the Deutsche Nationalbibliografie;
detailed bibliographical data can be found under:http://dnb.ddb.de

Series title and concept: Jürgen Tesch

© Prestel Verlag, Munich · Berlin · London · New York, 2004

Prestel books are available worldwide. Please contact your
nearest bookseller or oneof the following Presel offices for information
concerning your local distributor:

Prestel Verlag, Königinstrasse 9, 80539 Munich
Tel. +49 (89) 38 17 09-0, fax +49 (89) 38 17 09-35

Prestel Publishing Ltd., 4 Bloomsbury Place, London WC1A 2QA
Tel. +44 (020) 7323-5004, fax +44 (020) 7636-8004

Prestel Publishing, 900 Broadway, Suite 603, New York, NY 10003
Tel. +1 (212) 995-2720, fax +1 (212) 995-2733
www.prestel.com

Translated from the German by Rosie Jackson
Edited by Christopher Wynne
Design: Maja Kluy, Berlin
Origination: LVD, Berlin
Printing: Jütte-Messedruck, Leipzig
Binding: Kunst- und Verlagsbinderei, Leipzig

Printed in Germany on acid-free paper

ISBN 3-7913-3086-1